THE INVENTED MOTHER

New Women's Voices Series No. 175

poems by

Thea Goodman

Finishing Line Press
Georgetown, Kentucky

THE INVENTED MOTHER

ACKNOWLEDGMENTS

"Summer Novel" was published in *Coachella Review* in summer 2020

Publisher: Leah Huete de Maines
Editor: Christen Kincaid
Cover Art: Iris Bernblum
Author Photo: Eric Oliver
Cover Design: Elizabeth Maines McCleavy

Order online: www.finishinglinepress.com
also available on amazon.com

Author inquiries and mail orders:
Finishing Line Press
PO Box 1626
Georgetown, Kentucky 40324
USA

Table of Contents

Fontanel

Airborne, I send cocktails to the parents
of the screaming baby. The soft spot sounds
fragrant and earthy, a french goat's cheese.

Fontanel was every head. The bowl of skull,
dangerous to touch, new nerves, synapse,
blood pocketing lobes, a pomegranate.

My silent teen's favorite fruit, I gloat yet know
bones coalesce, delicacy never ends. A break in
connection is daily as hunger, cruel as first love,

now dead. The father sleeps. The mother rises,
shakes her ice, swims the aisle—smiles, she's
peripatetic, searching for the shore.

Irate infant, no one delivers you up the sludge,
all our bedtime sheets are cold, an isolette.
Legs spin a sundial on the desert mattress.

Each brain is fused, encased in shell. Speak
to me, underwater child, I hear you through
a sea dream I once knew, I know

you, I know you well.

Opposing Statements

Ice in the gutters, leak in the sash
in the broken house we retreat to the cellar.
    Reverse time-travel, word droplets return
    to thoughts, breathless to #grateful.

The day is only Monday, the week naive
deadlines and parties to reach. The gravity of limbs—
    Affirm me. I am #blessed. No fever soaks the night,
    no metronome in skull, tight carapace in shell chill.

Meticulous plans doom; We descend slowly.
Cable to soothe, a fat couch forgives. A rat
    startles in the transom, sees his reflection
    licks his hands one by one, smoothing his brows.

Disgusted, I look away, choose a show. Reservations
don't toggle in my calendar. I have nowhere to go.
    His theory of self: I will outlast you.
    An indictment: we live in the caul.

I tug my ragged, neighborly haircut—a tragedy—
We will return to all we know: Vain, clotted calendars—
    The rodent engages in *self care*.
    in house-arrest underworld, I'm almost sure he's there.

Two Figures Hiking

A dire sentence to renew-

Clouds hover like clues.
Mashed potato shadows
glide over burnt hills.
Palm trees discuss
bikinis and margaritas not
my spraign-able ankle, your

bra that digs, my fallible bones, your—

what is it, seared deep
with scenery and diagnosis?
Tell the experts I loved you since
you were born, head coned, melting
sugar in the scalp. My pressure fell,
the placenta gleamed in a metal bowl,
your father's face minted green.

I would leave you too soon—now

words are a meager vise—*not a daughter,*
mother breaking, un-elastic, they/he—
when you are merely every word,
the cosmic meal, never

out of mind. I eat you, see? And you, me.

Devour. Stay and feast- the cloud cover
is quenching shade. Pissed, you hike
in front, kicking up what I heed, baby,

desert dust that swirls like advice.

Bones of Dead Pronouns

They found a skeleton on the train track
mingled with pine and sap. A waft of brie,
the fish store did not see the dead doe.

A gothic drive stowed pieces into purse
with coins, sand, bandaids. They appliquéd a skull
on the Japanese tote I once bought in Berkeley.

Under the bones pricked a rose embroidery.
Their early pink idea: stitched beauty
tight bud, green leaf, onto the brown satchel.

The object names keep shifting strange
yet one is enough for the everything we carry:
The bag held Pez, cheddar Goldfish, Golden Books,

tickets for a foreign train, even their tooth
that fell out at school. I stare as they drip
Joy on the bones and I offer bleach. But

Clorox degrades the bones. They'll disintegrate.
Can you please leave? I can but—I remember
the hose splitting the sun, my thumb on the nozzle, high

shrieks of summer, when they were a girl.

The New Lover

It's a pact. The pain redder than the yellow
the green scent lighter than almost-April.
Released from the ward, I ride up the lake
fingering pamphlets about formula.
Blue shimmy over the not-an-ocean,
the scent of soil warms into the spring car.
New baby mummy-tight in plastic seat,
rose cheeks pout like the Buddha.
Home, a chair is produced, a hand on my elbow,
I sink. Headrest cradles hair, an odor of
oats and blood. Baby on the floor
expecting nothing. Cozy, wretched
beginner, younger now than two days ago
when labor began. The backward ricochet,
rare light tunneling to an unknown mother
raveling. A revelation. The baby knows
nothing. Dictates everything. No
language. Failing memory rushes bloom
on tongue. Up from my crib. A yellow room
the way the West Village trees budded
popcorn for a slim and irascible week,
the tease of their perfume wafting through
the door of the diner to the new lover,
a stranger swaddled in the faux leather banquette.

As Soon as My Husband Leaves I Smoke and Drink

the war is— I cannot speak a knife slit under ribs

obscene hunger greed flowered sheets breakfast ceiling caving in

the war is she sleeps he leaves the war is men take

my father my son no light is to steal, is stolen

the war is a blindfold I cannot see the war is I know

a subterranean sheaf

is back to back I cannot hear deaf father dense heart

a hospital no beeps is to weep

morning breath I cannot *not* smell the war is a double negative

is my daughter my son a boy I could eat   the war

is to flee suddenly a refugee

is newspapers I cannot read the language I don't speak

the war is fire in kitchen window no news, no TV is

an insecure signal I cannot breathe the war is first words night baby

bye tree sky I cannot be the war is he left his razor

accidental cut neglect hit spree the war is yoke

is violence frozen pipes burst

the war is explosion   is nineteen   babies in a cellar

is   I cannot—   touch

is   unspeakable   is you is me is rain

is I cannot change   the bed no clean sheets

the war is   I love

                                I am not free

the war is my children   I cannot see   the war is the will to

overpower is he is we   the war is the word *war*   the word *world*

is hiding   a rubbled lot   a crushed school is broken

is never won is   is disempower   break branch

tree   is time passing and fixed

fake calendars   snow   to leaf

the war is men laughing   on a death beach   is winter here forever

is you is me

After

June, 2020

I died early on and am a tourist on earth.
A visitor, I eat your risotto with spring peas
and moan. And I cry at each shot.

A glut of beauty, hellebores in your yard
face the soil, shyly. Inside, a clog in the duct,
the straight line of your love. Your curiosity

about the numbers, my resistance, tension
rising story a breakable glitter.
Babies tight like summer rolls,

powerfully neat before they scream.
The spring drops white petals hot
snow upon limestone pavers that smell like

sex. Dirty socks, she said. But we like it.
The everything we inhale, the before and after
scent of oyster sheen on inner thigh.

Meditate

The dropping in is automatic
disavow the acrobatic.
Circle of breath, a birth right.

(He ate his breakfast at a diner.)

The body a rising float
above newsprint, flannel flowers,
ignorant chintz. A wife's origami shoulders.

(Wanting to be alone.)

Peonies splash across a headboard,
myopic lines against the grain
to peeing standing up,

(His eggs slide into a green glass cup.)

The sound of rain—then stop.
Age eight, a breathing gravitas, float light
rose wallpaper, wake and dress

(He wore a pinstripe suit,)

upon rising. Outfits for flight,
secure barrettes, a skirt with zippers,
shoes almost tight.

(black wingtips.)

Deride easy answers. Walk past their door
the way to flight is breath like stone
the cold above.

Before

November, 2019

Sanctuary yet—

broken sky hangs over your
single daffodil. Winter chill
helicopter interrupting yellow,
as she sits at a round table
studying geometry.

Inside, the fig tree presses at the wall
aching to touch the skylight.
Your daughter rips a cuticle,
surprises you: asks for a hug.

Pink cardboard covers the hole,
November's warning,
forty mile-per-hour winds popped
a skylight. The glass rectangle
flew and shattered the night.

The next day you collected the pieces,
icy platelets, heavy prismatic cracked
storm glass littering the milk alley
as a coyote prowled the school's playground.

Early March 2020

Not one coyote prowling
the school, but a pack, eating
the heads off the pink tulips
and administrative boxwoods.

Molting daffodils and leeks,
cold ankles, too thin jacket,
makes memory of new clothing
smoke of desire and cigarettes

on Eighty-sixth Street, smooth
apples of our unlined cheeks
to an orchard in Queens
and my grandfather whistling gay
hands cutting forsythia.

Swimming

After the Bat Mitzvah, faded October tan, mercury rising, I go for a
swim

questions loom turquoise
lake breaks rock   stories of light
open and shift   a family poses in a row

                         reproduction

is magical and a trope

is—
our story—yet alone I swoon

                    scalp unstitched in urban ice bath

    open water threatens breath   dense velvet strokes no bottom

a confused goose shits green and struts

                    his task clean, unlike the new mother nursing
self-consciously on the bank

look at her: a book splayed untouched beside her
The Divine—

the utterly *common*   the divided effort was mine!
Imagine this:

temple teen said goodbye to childhood and
                                    met God

an abstraction in a crevasse—or that cloud, *there*, or—

                    the lake's nuanced rock face no foothold gradient
floats of wrapper and leaf

autumn hues of not knowing. Abrading flesh up mossy tetnus

dry myself off with the bad towel- lick lips for salt- there's none
blank

return to my family and cook
a blue box of pasta   devoid of minutes

in the big house   of no idea

Berkeley View

1
Today archipelagos
curve with curiosity
clumped with trees
unseen possibilities
serious mysteries.
Dark clouds gather and crush
the movement of fog
highlight the crisp punctuation
of cypress and pine.

2
Each day is your attempt.
Put feet in place of iphone,
crash away dull connections,
hone sharp ones,
like mother, father, sister,
daughter and son.

3
Visitors are coming.
Stand it as hot as you can:
Greet them in matching caftans,
even adorn the children, and use rhetoric
thrown out after the sixties, *Sacred
Mother.*

4
You nursed for nineteen months,
sitting braless in a dining chair, glamorous
neighbor, borrowing milk, asking
if you'd ever get dressed again.

5
Now pass the lemon tree and strut.
The children are ensconced in tales of Krishna,
the community meeting awaits.
The storyteller wears a dashiki.
The children are laughing, their father knows
how to cook and take them to karate.

No Accidents

A lone coyote was spotted at the children's school,
you've heard. Languorous by the steel swing set,
licking the slide, hating math—

Anchors say it's funny
but the symptoms are hardly subtle.
In the future, animals disorient
cows wander into town.

In the debate a vegan rushed the stage—
invisible methane clogs pastoral air.
Asymptomatic droplets halo mom-brains—
and hover behind the candidate, a reaper.

The wife of the candidate becomes a lion,
—incisors sharp in the still—
but she can't fight drifting ice floes,
or the cat who kills cardinals,

proudly delivering the uncut strand of intestine.
Nothing trickled down. The signs
were always heavy handed, even showy,
blood scattered in snow.

Show me your screen
cleaned with non-abrasive cloth.
Don't scratch a smile into the reflection.

Famous Mother

My mother had a portrait painted, did your mother have one?
No, she wasn't—
It was commissioned. It hung in this frame here.
That's a mirror.
We cut the canvas out of the frame and replaced it with a mirror.

> We look in the mirror, remembering our mothers
> yolked before words, nascent latch and drift.

I just felt like every time I entered the house, my mother was staring
down at me. It was odd.
So you put a mirror in the frame—

> A siskin calls. (I know bird names from her poems.)
> Another answers.

We liked the frame.
So now you're staring at yourself.
I guess I am!
> Laughter warbles our reflection.
> A woodpecker drills and drills.
> I catch her eye in the mirror.
> A lightwave stitches yearning
> between us. She tucks blonde hair
> behind her ear. Delicacy of fingertip—
> inherited elegance—

What did you do with the actual painting? The portrait of your
mother?
There she is!

> she says, pointing at her reflection.
> We crack up, high with my ludicrous
> pelvic floor, her problematic sinuses.
> Her feathered iris darts the rim, refusing to settle.

Wings—maybe a junco, maybe a dove—take flight.
Between us a snapping rush as our eyes meet
and register decades, unsung mysteries, who
they were, who we are.

Sixteen

Beneath the lip of the day
       (The cells turn over every seven years)
I gathered string beans in a pile,
snipped tips, checked phone,
and called you.
       (Nine was your age of no tomorrows
       perfection in chess memory and teeth)
You didn't answer, I seared the ginger, I
added mushroom and basil.
       (Limbs like rolled marble, fresh steamed
       rice of head, you turned—made a wish)
Turns out you were at a party, a world of puppets
in drindle skirts flipped inside-out
from flowers to migraines, complex ideation.
       (The semesters were a favorite blanket, clean
       and pilled. Shredding at satin seams)
Thin sliced scallion, added soy, the day's sun
dipping, darkening to end of Autumn.
       (At thirteen the metal rectangle landed
       in your palm, you took endless selfies)
When ballads croon my eyes tear,
I'm not old, but I know what it means: my bilious
entreaty, your natural evasion, my distrust of screens.
       (Costumes acclimate to the dark, you
       do what I don't know)
The dish is hot for Saturday night.

Advanced Maternal Age

At the deep end of possibility
a pencil dot floats in a pelvic pool.
The teenagers say there's nothing to do.
Potato chips' salt solace won't outlast

the pebble in your shoe. They lick their lips
and sigh. Travel to town for a hacked green
coconut. Imaginary bones grew.
The prodigal egg drop always felt new.

Eschew the age of no tomorrows. Pout
into straws of bamboo. Their masks down, dirty
to dye sky blue with complaint. They'll never
perish. Unwrap your medicine and chew.

Time goes in two directions, a tide sifts,
divides. Sit in the middle at zero.

Summer Novel

Done, stand in the woods
pages behind you
insects screaming
like nothing has happened.

(A bottle slips from your hand
Beer into peat, the trees
in German beer gardens
relish their hops.
leaves grow dense and shady)

It feels like a book,
thumbs scrolling through time
as if the screen is liquid,
and the characters are impossibly
relatable.

(Pour the whole bottle out into the ground.
No need for the blurring.)

Behind you the house is lit
chapters snapping like magna tiles,
slices of yellow and orange,
warm the rooms,
plexiglass attachments,
coming together with relief.

(Leave the bottle there
It's degradable, and your own yard.
An awning of delectable shade will
shelter you. Sand will return
all the pages
will vanish.)

Hand on the knob,
return to the living
more and less human.
The children are sleeping,
you haven't said goodnight.

Vintage Summer Sale

1. At the end of the world sale
the clothing is penniless,
mannequins stripped bare.
Relativity is filigreed dust
because bull markets rush.
Lungs harden and fail.
The beach erodes ledged
with stairs. We've seen it before,
never learned how to share.

2. The patterns align but
getups collapse, sweat through silk
ripped lining, moth-eaten collar,
wedges of grift sort sand between
people who cannot touch. Skin
carrots on Mondays, a day to begin
again. Remember the turn of the century
miracle refugees. Ours, a tailor,
bolted fabric to rib. Eyes to lips.
Clothing wrecked, never forget how to kiss.

Family Yoga

The asanas were nothing less than love.
The body, a shell of who he was-

Mad men of sixty-two, dream world
domination, a boss's desk and title, the girl

she was big hair, mousse, white socks
name the place she can't abide—

Spooning blind, pretend to sleep.
Affable poses, hiding sheets.

Invitations, cutting teeth.
Heart-opening in Tulum?

Teacher's northern fleece
presses at his knees. In memory

she levitates and shifts
euphoria and drift.

Upside-down the earth is new.
King blankets cover and reveal

insight shocks: *a tuning fork shines.*
Rebellion is never or soon.

Savasana, then guacamole.
Fermented mango margarita at noon.

Thirst

Abandon the salt mine in Chile,
run from an avalanche of stone
the white impervious to heat.
My son licks the mountain
we ascend and takes shade on the blue
bus, left petrified in 1930: icy
cokes, the guide's thermos of matcha,
walls graffitied with timeless obscenity,
bottled water, pretending plastic
is not permanent, blue curl of label
tearing love. The miners, left their houses
made of salt, each day. Nine thousand miles
above the sea, women carved chairs out
of the mineral, a playful chaise, for fainting.
Thirst quenched, he ascends with me on salt staircase—
that sloughs crystals with each step, sweat my
baby, we all evaporate to a temple of sky.

Summer Lens

Sailboats clanged over the bay's
surface of spaghetti and *affairs*,
the words I heard, *bright*
but not *intellectual.*

A *vichysoisse* and that
beloved salad. Carrots,
lemon and raisin. Station
father on the landing,

mother's engine idling
and *miffed* to splinters on
the dock, barnacles below,
a mussel to disgust,

a ghost petrifies. Her
old modeling mannequin
rising, abandoned.
Wet the bed then cry,

her figure in the doorway
hush. Later shush of toothbrush
on bone. Check, but no one's there
mint stains the air.

Heat everlasting, peek and see,
Mother behind a swinging door,
hips in a row on a wicker settee,
white wine shining in the glass,

cigar smoke wafting up the stair,
grown ups howling on the porch,
the distance from here to there.

With Thanks

I am grateful to Leah Huete de Maines for choosing The Invented Mother as a finalist in the New Women's Voices Chapbook Competition 2022 and Kevin Maines and Christen Kincaid for shepherding it to publication. Thank you, Elaine Sexton, superb teacher and author. Thank you, Kevin Pilkington, Luke Taylor, Mary Karr, Liza Hudock, Emily Walters, Diana Arterian, Emily Gray Tedrowe, Gina Frangello, Zoe Zolbrod, Rebecca Makkai, Rachel De Woskin, Dika Lam, Elise Paschen, Vanessa Smith, Marlena Baraf, Jennifer Stewart Miller, Bonnie Jill Emanuel, Nell Freudenberger, Paul Logan, Sarah Hammerschlag, Suzanne Buffam, Wendy Gimbel, Elizabeth Schmidt, Jane Wagman, Susanna Felleman, Hope Litoff, Susan Augustine, Daniel Sutherland, Elizabeth Kieff, Tom Levinson, Ryan Coyne, Zayd Dohrn, Brenda and Dave Bergen, Max Ryan, Niamh King, Jennifer Pope, Jennifer Desmond, John Berg, Jasanna and John Britton, Claudia Swan, Gabriel Presler, Yoshi Yamada, Romi Crawford, Hal Kugeler, Dodi Wexler, Ed Flood, Iris Bernblum, Monica Rezman, Dianna Frid, Janelle Savage and Chris and Fiona Farrell. Your energy, art, love and support ignite my brain and heart. To the extended Goodman and Oliver/Sivcoski families, thank you for believing in me and standing by. Eric, Ethan and Martin, my deepest gratitude for each of you; you are my heart.

Thea Goodman is poet, novelist, educator and a finalist in The New Women's Voices Chapbook Competition 2022 by Finishing Line Press. Her previous poems appeared in *The Brooklyn Review* and *The Coachella Review*. She is the author of *The Sunshine When She's Gone* (Henry Holt and co. 2013) a critically acclaimed novel about a marital crisis that ensues upon a child's birth. Goodman's short fiction and essays have appeared in journals such as *Story, The New England Review, Confrontation, Columbia, Arrowsmith* and *The Rumpus* among others, and received a Pushcart Prize Special Mention. She earned The *Columbia* Fiction Award, a *Story* Magazine Award and inclusion in The New York Public Library's Digital Archive, *Stories on The MTA*, 2019 for her short story, "Evidence." Goodman received a BA at Sarah Lawrence College and an MFA at Brooklyn College, CUNY. She has taught writing at several universities, and was a Visiting Faculty Member at the University of Chicago between 2016-2019. *The Invented Mother* is her first book of poems. Born in New York City, she now lives in Chicago with her family.